Models from Junk

D1795267

Would you like to make a dragon or
a puppet, build a rocket or a train?
Or perhaps construct a gay market
scene or a merry-go-round? With the
help of the simple instructions in this
book you can have fun creating these
and many other models and
creatures out of the old boxes, milk
bottle tops, and bits and pieces to
be found in every home.

Cover design by Brenda B. Jackson

THINGS YOU WILL NEED....

....AND SOME OTHERS.

Models from Junk

Brenda B. Jackson

Evans Brothers Limited London

Published by Evans Brothers Limited
Montague House, Russell Square,
London, WC1

First published 1971
Third printing 1974

Set in 12 on 14 point Baskerville
Printed in Great Britain by Cox & Wyman
Ltd., London, Reading and Fakenham
CSD. ISBN 0 237 35199 4   PRA3585
PB. ISBN 0 237 35200 1

Introduction

Before you start making some of the things shown in this book, here are some points that might help you.

Firstly, it is important to remember that although the instructions tell you how to make the models it is a good idea to try and use the instructions only as a guide to help you to invent your own objects. Sometimes you might think of a better way of making a particular model – try it. Do not try to copy the decorations shown in the drawings carefully. Think of your own designs for decoration. Remember as well that the models can be any size. The size will depend on the boxes or other materials that you use.

Secondly, make sure that you have a good collection of odds and ends such as pebbles, boxes, cardboard, bits of wool and coloured paper, beads, twigs, cotton reels, etc. Try to get into the habit of collecting these things but remember to store them neatly. Get some old carrier bags or boxes, label them and just put things into them as you find them.

Thirdly and finally, try to keep a small sketchbook with you all the time. Note down in drawing and note form things that might be useful when designing your own models – an interesting tree or rock, an old broken wrecked car, a shell, patterns from a butterfly or an old stone wall – record them all in your sketchbook.

I hope you will enjoy making the models described and shown but most of all I hope this book will encourage and help you to invent and make things of your own.

Brenda B. Jackson

Contents

Using boxes

You will need

Boxes of all kinds – round, square, oblong, large and small. Stiff card, hardboard. Glue, scissors, sticky tape. Paper, plain or coloured, crepe and tissue. Scraps of fabric of all kinds. Matches and matchboxes. Plasticine or clay. Pencils, crayons, paints and brushes. Beads, buttons, pulses such as dried beans or rice.

Using milk bottle tops

You will need

Plenty of milk bottle tops. Polystyrene blocks. Stiff card, hardboard, strawboard. Silver foil. Stiffened hat bases or old hats. Small saw, old metal knitting needle. Dressmakers' pins, scissors. Needle and strong thread. Glue. Old nylon stockings. Feathers, cotton wool, beads. Paints, brushes, pencils, crayons.

Using egg boxes

You will need

Plenty of egg boxes. Pieces of wood, hardboard, card. Boxes of all sizes. Nails, hammer, scissors. Strong wire, stones, bits of fabric. Dressmakers' pins, old knitting needles, needle and thread. Glue, paints, brushes, Plasticine. Large strong hairpins. Sticky tape, coloured paper.

Using fabric scraps

You will need

Large boxes, stiff card. Paints and brushes, pencils. Coloured crepe paper, stiff paper. Sea shells, small pebbles. Fabric of all kinds, ribbon. Cotton wool, buttons, beads, milk bottle tops, sequins, feathers. Needle, thread, scissors. Pipe cleaners, elastic, scraps of wool. Old nylon stockings, old gloves. Stiff wire, pieces of wood, hammer, nails. Stiffened hat bases or old hats. Thick rug wool. Plasticine.

Using small machine bits

You will need

Boxes of many sizes, including shoe boxes. Pebbles, glue, Plasticine. Old watches, clocks, small machine parts. Nails, screws, knitting needles, dressmakers' pins. Stiff wire, thread, string. Paints and brushes. Scraps of fabric, small buttons, beads, pulses. Yoghurt or cream cartons.

Using cardboard rolls

You will need

Cardboard rolls of all lengths and sizes. Cheese boxes, shoe boxes, small boxes. Paper, stiff card, cardboard. Glue, sticky tape. Matches, scraps of balsa wood, string. Needle, cotton, thread, scissors. Paints and brushes. Scraps of fabric, twigs. Thin wire, dressmakers' pins, strong hairpins.

Using paper plates

You will need

Paper plates in various sizes. Stiff card, coloured tissue paper. Scissors, paints and brushes. Glue, sticky tape. Ribbon, thin wire, feathers, net. Milk bottle tops. Plasticine or clay. Pins, or stapling machine.

Using boxes

Omnibus

A. Take a large oblong box.

B. Cut out two pieces of card, larger than the box, in the shape shown in diagram 2, and stick one piece to each side of the box.

C. Make the wheels from cheese boxes by drawing the pattern of the spokes on to the boxes and painting them. Stick these to the main box.

D. The driver can be made of clay and painted or dressed with fabric scraps.

E. The driver's seat is made by taking a small box and sticking on pieces of card, as shown in diagram 5, to make the sides and foot step. This can be stuck to the main coach body.

F. The coach can now be painted. Make sure you paint some people sitting at the windows.

1.

2.

3.

4.

5.

6.

Using boxes

A Pleasure Boat

A. Firstly take four boxes and remove the lids. Glue the boxes together to make the lower deck of the ship, the open ends facing you.

B. On to the top of this row of boxes glue a strip of stout card.

C. Take another group of boxes, glue them together in the same way, making the top deck of the boat.

D. On to these stick one big box to make the captain's look-out.

E. The funnels can be made of rolls of card which are stapled or fixed with sticky tape on to the roof of the look-out.

F. Make pieces of furniture out of odd scraps of fabric, matches, matchboxes, etc. and figures from clay or Plasticine and furnish each of the rooms.

G. To finish off the boat cut out pieces of card, add portholes and stick these on to the sides of the boat on the lower deck. Use crumpled up crepe and tissue paper to make the sea.

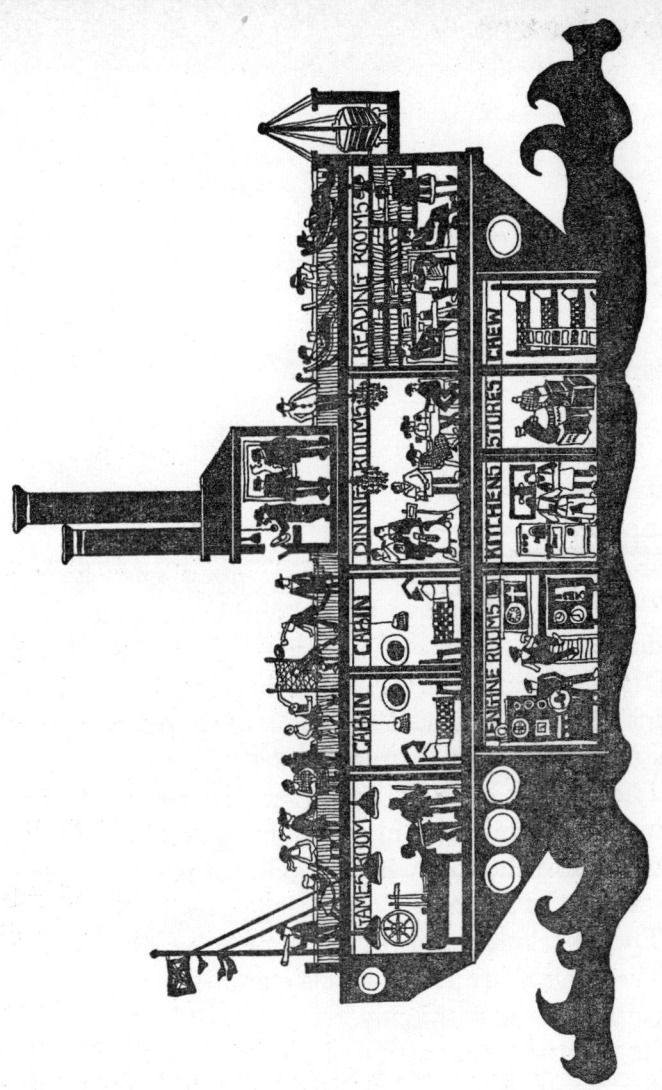

13

Using boxes

A Market

A.   Take a box. Remove the lid and one side as shown in diagram 1.

B.   Draw a street scene showing houses and shops on the inside of the box. Cut out the roof shapes and paint the street scenes as in diagram 2.

C.   The market stalls (diagram 3) can be made from a matchbox tray with four matches glued into the corners to support the roof which is made of paper. Some of the stalls could be made of small ring boxes.

D.   The wheels are made of circles of firm card.

E.   The figures are made of clay and dressed in pieces of cloth stuck on to the clay.

F.   Small beads, tiny strips of paper, buttons, beans, rice, etc. can be used to show the different sorts of goods on sale.

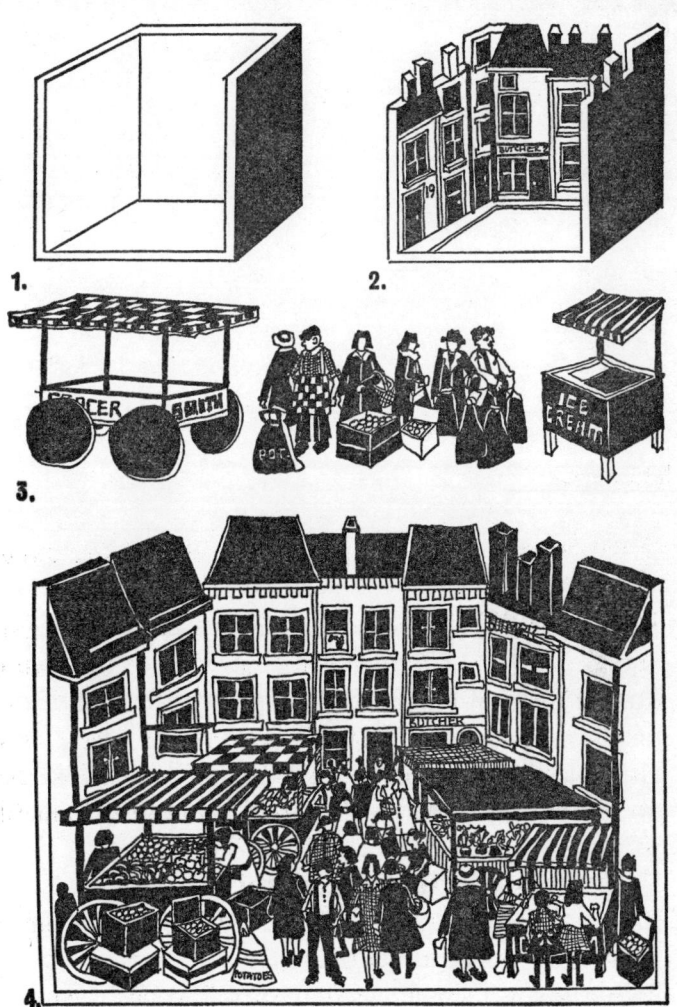

1.

2.

3.

4.

Using boxes

Turtles and Tortoises

A. Take a piece of hardboard and sketch the outline of the tortoise shapes.

B. Make a collection of round cheese boxes and small square boxes. Paint them with brightly coloured paints.

C. Keep one box for the 'head' of each tortoise.

D. Build up the body shape of each tortoise by sticking the boxes on to the hardboard.

E. Paint the spaces in between the boxes.

F. You could also use beads, buttons, beans, rice, etc. for extra pieces of pattern.

A.

B.

C.

D.

Using boxes

An Early Railway Train

A. Arrange a group of boxes as shown in diagram 1. Glue them together. The bigger boxes will be the engine and carriages. The small boxes are to make sure that the train will stand steadily. These are glued to the bottom of the larger boxes and should be hidden by the wheels when the model is finished.

B. Make the 'plate' (diagram 2) by cutting out the shape in card and sticking it on to the boxes in one long strip.

C. The wheels are made of round cheese boxes and glued firmly to the 'plate'.

D. The figures in the open carriages are made of Plasticine or clay.

E. The chimney is made of a paper roll stapled or fixed with sticky tape to the body of the engine.

F. The railway train can now be painted and decorated.

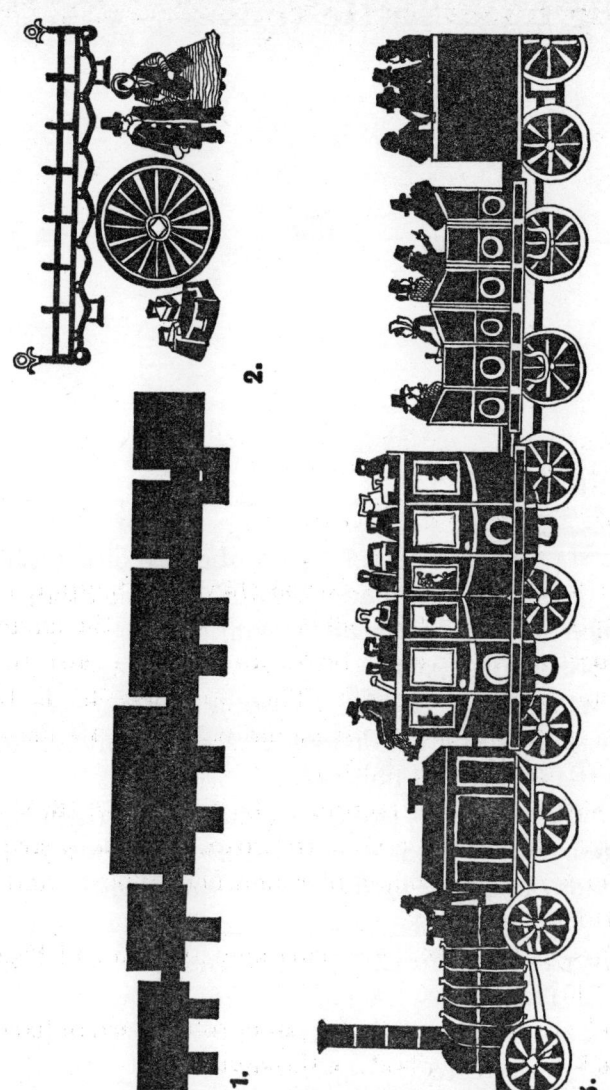

2.

1.

3.

Using milk bottle tops

A Fantastic Bird

A. First carve the rough shape of the bird out of a block of polystyrene as in diagram 1, using a small saw for the main shape and a heated metal knitting needle for the more detailed parts.

B. Start covering the bird with milk bottle tops, attaching them by pushing a dressmakers' pin firmly through the bottle top into the polystyrene.

C. The bird's comb is made of card and attached in the same way. Feathers, small puffs of cotton wool and beads can also be used for some of the details.

D. In this model the 'legs' are completely covered with silver foil. On top of this are pinned long strips of cut foil. This is very effective as the slightest breeze will make the strips flutter and shimmer reflecting the surrounding colours.

E. Make sure that no part of the model is too thin.

1.

2.

Using milk bottle tops

Helmet and Headdress

The Helmet

A. The basic shape of the helmet is a stiffened hat base, in this case the skull cap style. You can use an old straw hat, cut to shape.

B. Start by cutting out strips of card and covering them with silver foil. Staple or sew these along the centre of the hat base from back to front to make the spokes.

C. Milk bottle tops are now sewn or stapled all over the skull cap.

The Headdress

A. The basic shape for the headdress is also a stiffened hat base but, in this case, it has been given extra height by sticking pieces of cotton wool on to the hat. The cotton wool can be kept in place by putting a piece of old nylon stocking over the entire hat base. Milk bottle tops are sewn all over the headdress.

B. The forehead fringe is made of milk bottle tops hanging from individual threads.

C. The cascades at the sides are made of milk bottle tops hanging on single threads. Some of these can be painted.

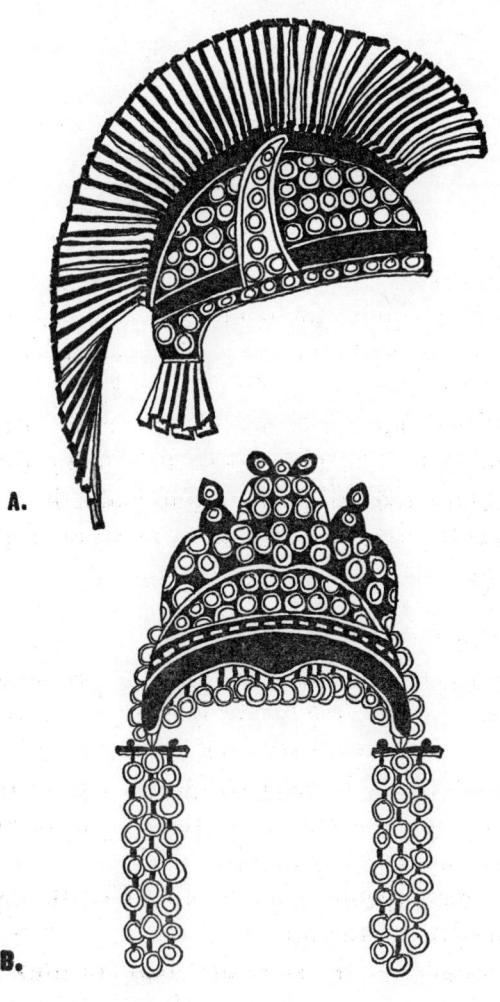

A.

B.

Using milk bottle tops

A Silver Knight

A. First sketch your design roughly on to a sheet of board. Strawboard or hardboard is suitable.

B. Working from the top of the design, cover a small area at a time with a strong glue such as Marvin, and start sticking the milk bottle tops firmly on to the adhesive.

C. In this design the background has been painted black, so have some parts of the knight, for example the legs. The outline shape of the figure was left unpainted.

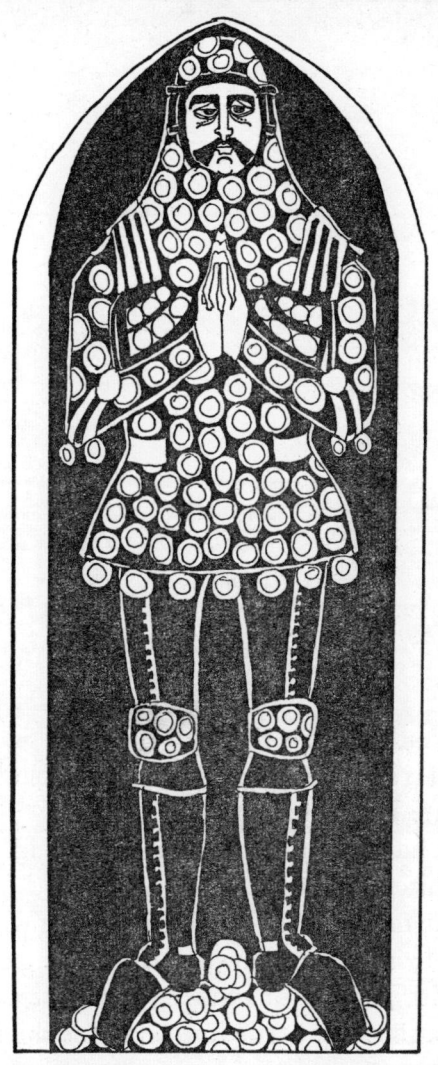

Using milk bottle tops

Shields

A. First cut out the basic shape of the shield in stiff card. If the shield is going to be used in a school play, it might be better to make it of hardboard.

B. Paint the background colour of the shield. It could be black, white or silver.

C. Sketch the design on to the shield using a wax crayon.

D. Working from the top downwards, cover a small area at a time with Marvin or other strong adhesive and gradually stick the milk bottle tops on to the shield, following your crayon design.

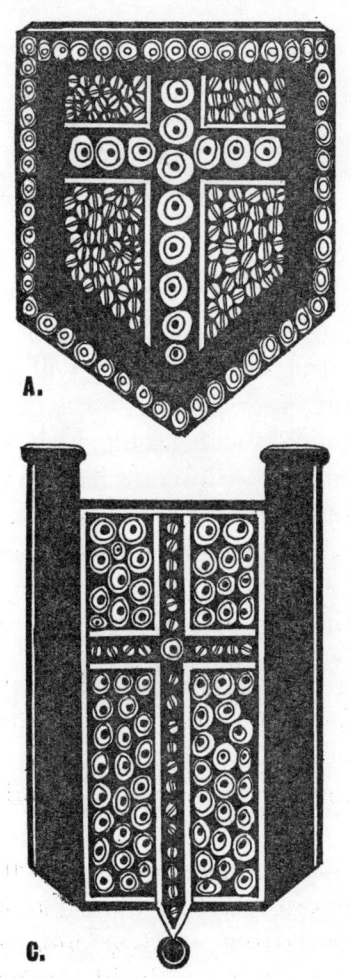

A.

C.

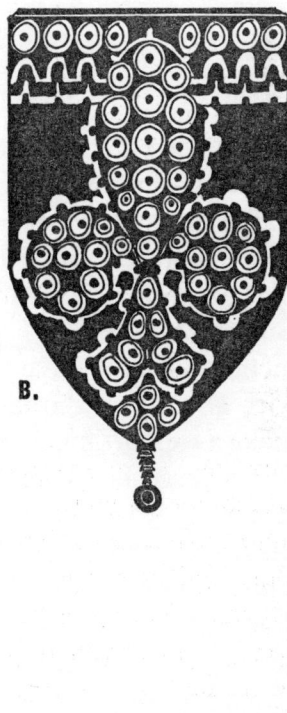

B.

Using egg boxes

A Dragon

A. If you want to make the dragon fairly big it will need some sort of internal support.

B. Nail a piece of wood, two inches wide by one inch deep (the length will be decided by the dragon's height) to a piece of hardboard, as in diagram 1.

C. Cut out two strips of hardboard slightly wider than 2 inches and nail these to the timber. Nail some strong wire about two thirds of the way along the timber to make a support for the arms (see diagram 2).

D. Put a large box over the wood and fill the box with stones. This will keep the model steady. In diagram 3 the front of the box has been removed to show the stones. This large box will also make the 'haunches' of the dragon.

E. Stick the egg boxes on to this structure.

F. Thread the boxes on to the wire 'arms' making sure they rest on the dragon's knees.

G. Use old knitting needles, dressmakers' pins, bits of fabric, etc. for extra decorations.

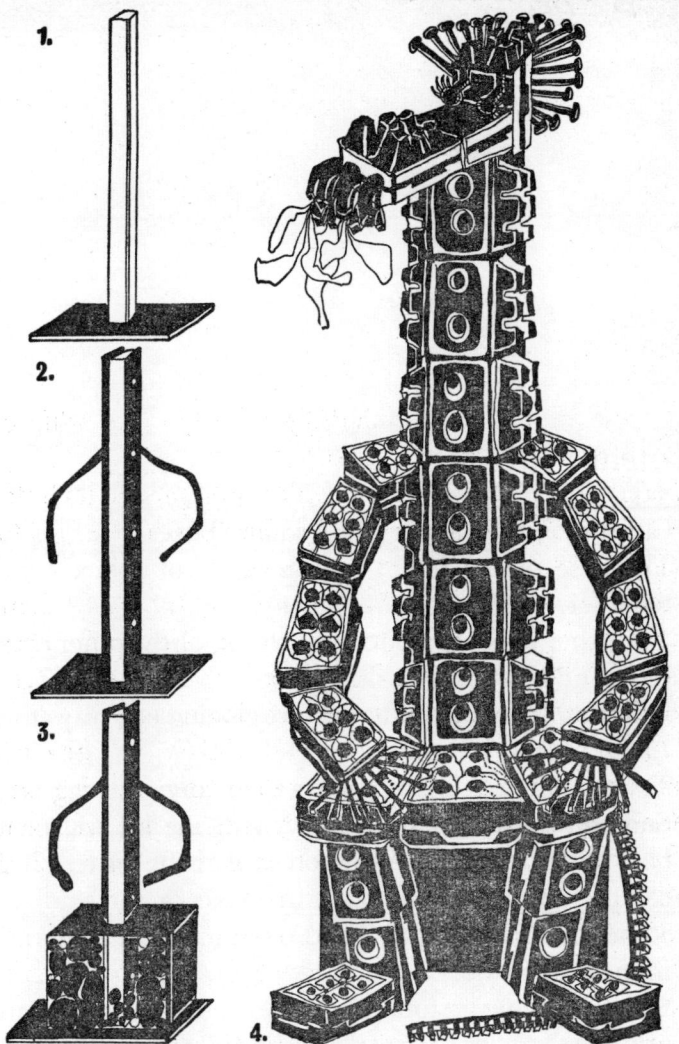

Using egg boxes

A Totem Pole

A. Collect together about 5 or 6 square boxes.

B. The base of the totem pole is made of 2 boxes glued together.

C. The other boxes are piled one on top of the other on this base, and glued into position.

D. Working from the bottom, start glueing egg trays to the totem pole.

E. Try to think of different ways to arrange the egg boxes. Sometimes show a front view with the lid still on the box, sometimes with the lid off so that the pattern inside can be seen, sometimes place the boxes on their sides.

F. Sometimes leave a space, and paint masks or patterns on to the totem pole.

G. On the top of the totem pole you could put a collection of brightly coloured masks or headdresses. These could be made of card.

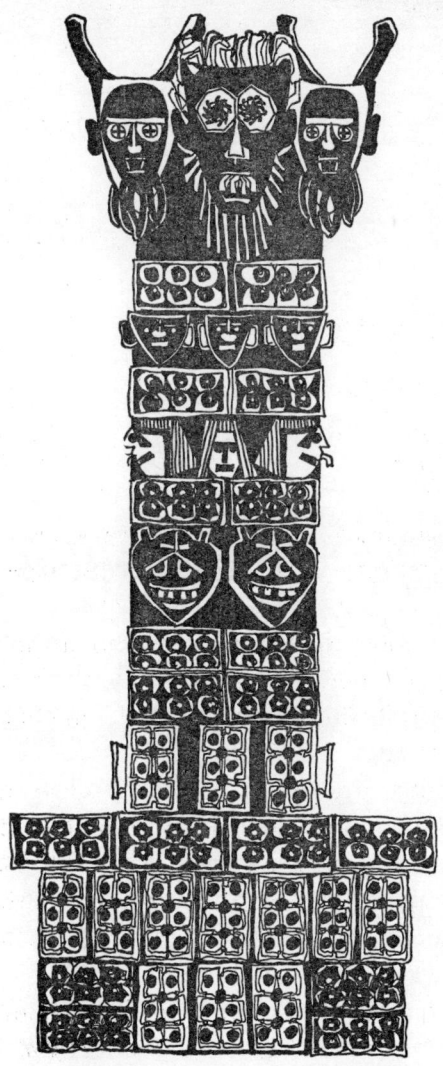

Using egg boxes

A Spikey Backed, Whiskered Creature

A. First collect together 5 or 6 egg boxes. Push the larger, stronger type of hairpins through the bottom of the boxes up to the hilt to make 'legs'. Seal the boxes tightly with sticky tape.

B. Thread a piece of stiff wire through all the boxes. Leave some sticking out of the last box to make the tail.

C. Along the backs of the boxes stick in dressmakers' pins to make the spikey back.

D. Make the shamrock-shaped feet out of pads of Plasticine. Stick the open ends of the hairpins into the Plasticine so that the creature will be able to stand up.

E. Paint the face. Use strips of coloured paper or thread for the creature's whiskers.

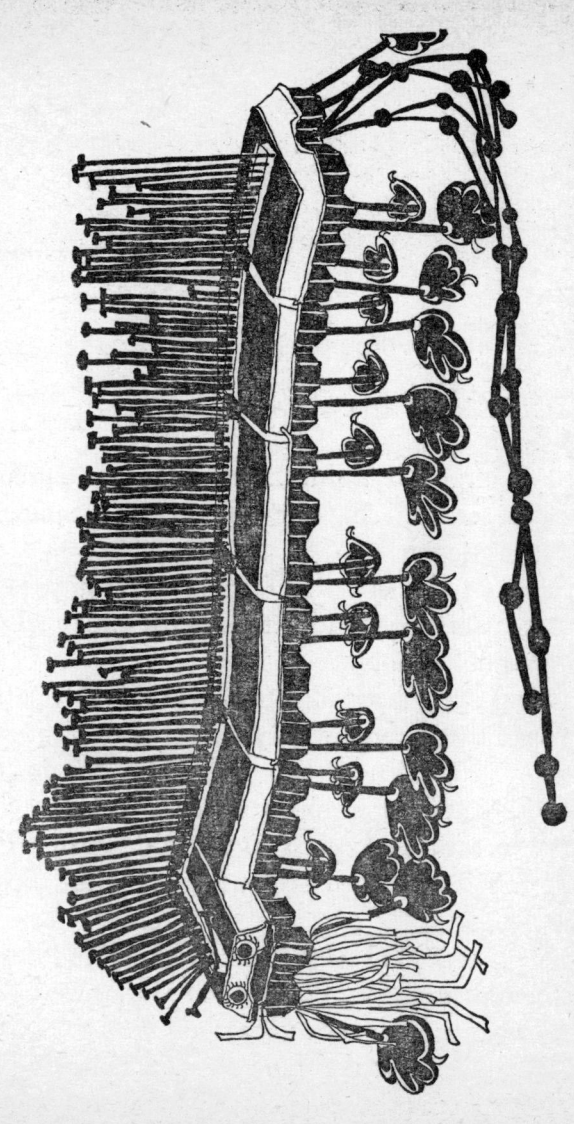

Using fabric scraps

A Fabric Fish Tank

A. Take a large box. Paint the inside blue and green.

B. Cut out seaweed shapes in coloured crepe paper and put these inside the box.

C. Make some sea shells out of crumpled stiff paper and put them in the box. Scatter these with some real shells and some small pebbles.

D. Cut out fish shapes in fabric. Sometimes the fabric can be brightly patterned and sometimes the material can be plain. You will need two pieces of fabric for each fish. Sew these together and stuff the fish shape with cotton wool or fabric scraps. You could decorate some of the fish shapes with buttons, beads, milk bottle tops, sequins, etc.

E. Attach a strand of strong thread to the middle of the fish and sew it to the roof of the box so that the fabric fish is suspended and appears to be swimming.

F. You could also make some sea anemones and small sea serpents from pipe cleaners.

1.

2.

3.ii.

3.i.

4.

5.

Using fabric scraps

Snakes

A. These snakes are very easy to make. First take an old nylon stocking and start packing it with old scraps of fabric or wool.

B. Push a stiffish wire into the stocking and finish the packing so that the fabric is around the wire.

C. Sew up the open end of the stocking.

D. Decorate the snake by sewing fabric or paper shapes on to the outside of the snake.

E. The eyes can be made with buttons or sequins and the fangs with wire.

F. Because of the wire stiffening you can bend and coil the snake into any position you like.

A.

B.

C.

Using fabric scraps

Wigs

The base for each of these wigs is a stiffened hat base which can be bought fairly cheaply in most department stores. You could use an old hat from which the brim has been cut.

Wig A
A. The black Egyptian 'hair' is made of strips cut from a piece of black material and then sewn on to the hat base. Velvet looks particularly good.
B. The headband, in a contrasting colour, is sewn on to the hat base at either side and on to the 'hair' at the front.
C. The snake charm band is made from plaited wire and overstitched on to the base.

Wig B
A. First draw the 'hair parting' on to the hat base.
B. Using thick rug wool sew the 'hair' along either side of the parting until the hat base is covered.
C. To make the ringlet bunches, first take an old glove and pack the 'fingers' with odd scraps of fabric.
D. Gather the end of the glove and tie a bright ribbon about it.
E. Now sew the 'bunches' on to either side of the wool-covered hat base.

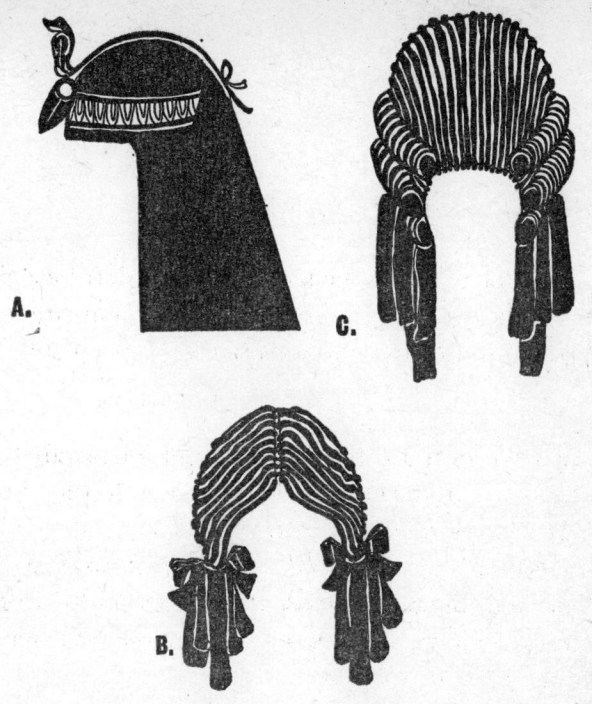

A.

C.

B.

Wig C

A. Cover the hat base with thick rug wool as in Wig B but this time the wool used for the hair should be sewn from front to back.

B. The bunches are also made in the same way as in Wig B.

C. To make the side curls, roll up strips of cloth tightly and then wind thick rug wool over each strip to cover it. The 'curls' are then sewn on to the sides of the hat base.

Using fabric scraps

Hand Puppet

A. Cut out two pieces of material roughly the shape shown in diagram 1 and large enough to cover your hand. Make one piece of material slightly larger than the other. This will become the back of the puppet.

B. Sew the two pieces together leaving the bottom end open. Thread thin elastic around the top of the fabric to make the 'neck'.

C. Make the 'mouth' by cutting out two pieces of card as shown in diagram 2. Sew these on to the 'head'.

D. On the bottom piece of card you could draw some teeth and a bright red tongue.

E. Make the ears, shown in diagram 3, from card or fabric.

F. Now decorate the puppet. Make the eyes with beads, the whiskers with lengths of stiff wire and tie a bright bow around the neck.

G. The puppet can be worked as shown in diagram 4.

1.

2.

3.

4.

5.

Using fabric scraps

Figures

A. First decide on the clothing, style, etc. of the figure.

B. Nail a length of wood to a block as shown in diagram 1. The length of the wood will depend on the height of the figure.

C. On to this wooden structure model a head in Plasticine.

D. Now wind wire about the wood as shown in diagram 2. The shape that the wire makes will depend on the style of the figure.

E. Cut out the clothes as shown in diagrams 3 and 4. You can paint plain fabric in bright colours.

F. Arrange these on to the front and back of the wire frame and sew up the sides.

G. Make hats, bags, etc. out of fabric scraps, feathers, wool, etc.

1. 2. 3. 4. 5.

Using small machine bits

A Robot

A. Take two shoe boxes and fill them with pebbles to make the 'feet' of the robot.

B. Use two more shoe boxes to make the legs.

C. On top of these place a large, square box making the 'body' of the robot.

D. Another box placed on the top of the 'body' makes the head.

E. Use strong glue to stick all the boxes together.

F. Now paint the robot.

G. You can now stick the machine pieces, with a strong glue such as Marvin, on to the boxes. You can use the inside bits of old watches and clocks and other small machine parts, nails, screws, knitting needles, dressmakers' pins, etc.

H. The arms are made by attaching a piece of wire to the sides of the body. The hands are made of nails, pins, etc.

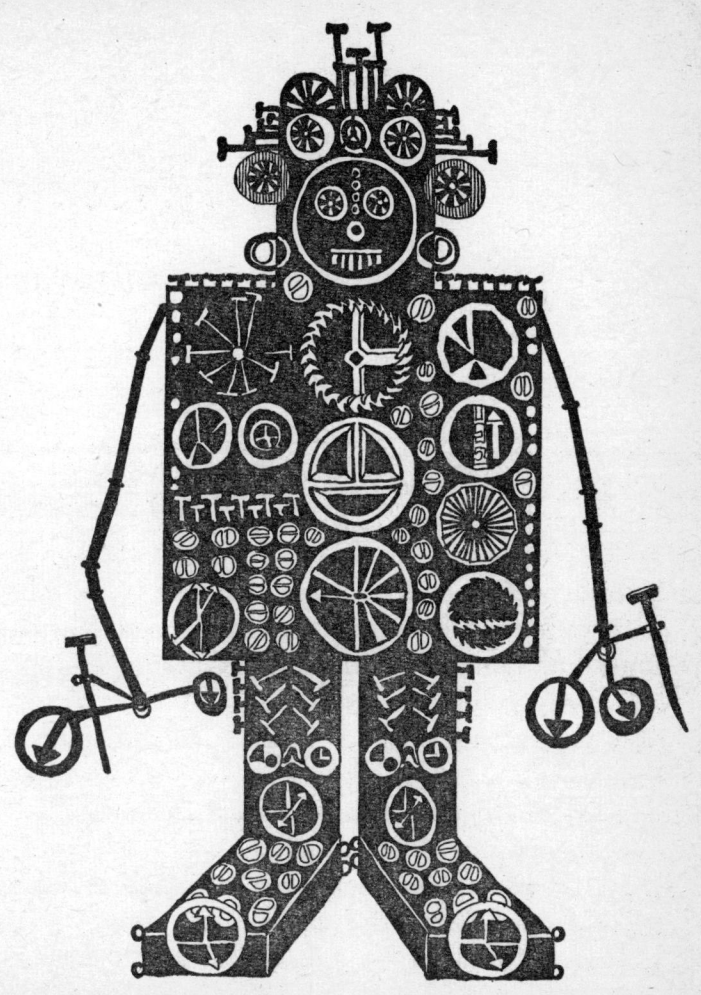

Using small machine bits

A Machine

A. Before you start to make your machine try to imagine what your machine is for. What goes in, and how does it come out? Work out all the things that *might* happen in between!

B. Now collect together a number of different sized boxes.

C. Group them together in a simple arrangement.

D. Glue them firmly to each other.

E. On to the box arrangement stick the machine bits, pins, needles, etc. Make the chutes with empty yoghurt cartons. Use strips of fabric, thread, string, small buttons, beads, beans, rice, dried peas, etc. for extra decoration.

Using small machine bits

A Machine Pieces Collage

A. Take a long shallow box and pack it almost to the rim with Plasticine (see diagram 2).
B. Start building up the pattern by pressing the machine bits firmly into the Plasticine.
C. You could also wind pieces of wool or thread around some of the machine pieces making more shapes.

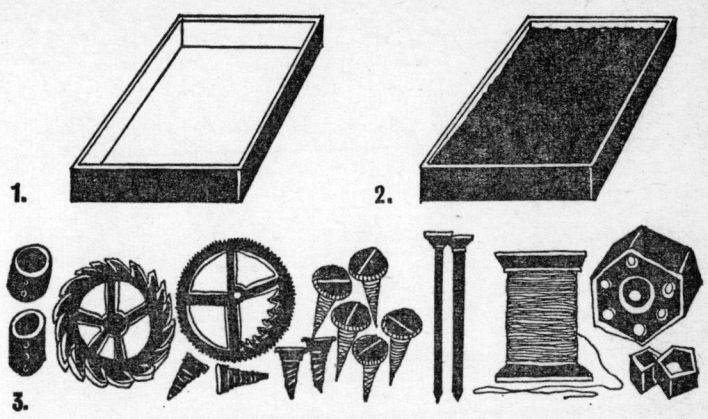

1. **2.**

3.

4.

Using cardboard rolls

A Puffing Billy

A. Take a thick stout cardboard roll as in diagram 1.

B. Now take a longer thinner tube and a smaller box and stick these three items together as shown in diagram 2. This will make the top part of the Puffing Billy – the striped part in the big drawing.

C. Cut out two strips of card to make the bottom (black) part of the model.

D. The wheels can be made out of stout cheese boxes and stuck on to the engine with glue.

E. Other parts can be built up with matches, bits of thread, and balsa wood and paper.

F. The main parts of the model can be painted brightly.

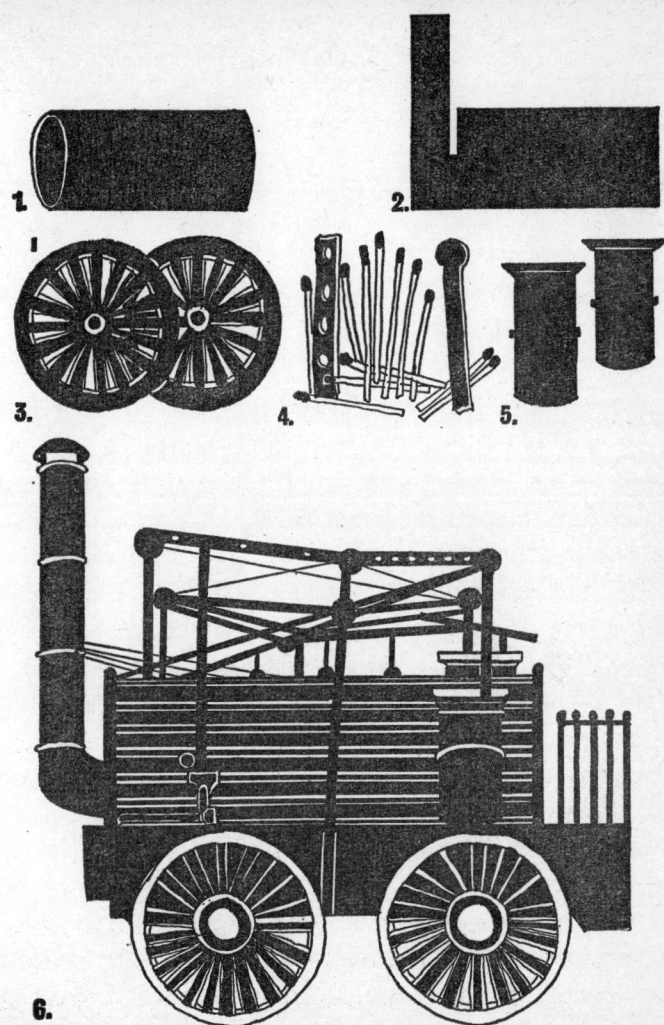

1.

2.

3.

4.

5.

6.

Using cardboard rolls

Witch on a Broomstick

A. Take four small thin cardboard rolls and one larger and thicker roll. Thread string through the rolls as shown in diagram 1. Remember to punch a hole at the end of each roll so that the string can be tied.

B. Paint a face on to the top part of the thicker roll. Sew or stick on wool for the hair and now dress the model using fabric scraps which can either be sewn or stuck on to the rolls.

C. Hands, shoes and hat can be made of cut paper (see diagrams).

D. The broomstick is made of a number of rolls stuck together with sticky tape, and twigs can be stapled or glued on for the 'brush'.

E. Thread pieces of string from a rod around the broomstick so that it hangs at an angle. Now attach the witch, sticking or stapling the figure by her clothing on to the broomstick, so that she is sitting firmly.

F. Hang the whole model so that it can move freely. It is best when suspended from the ceiling.

1.

2.

3.

4.

5.

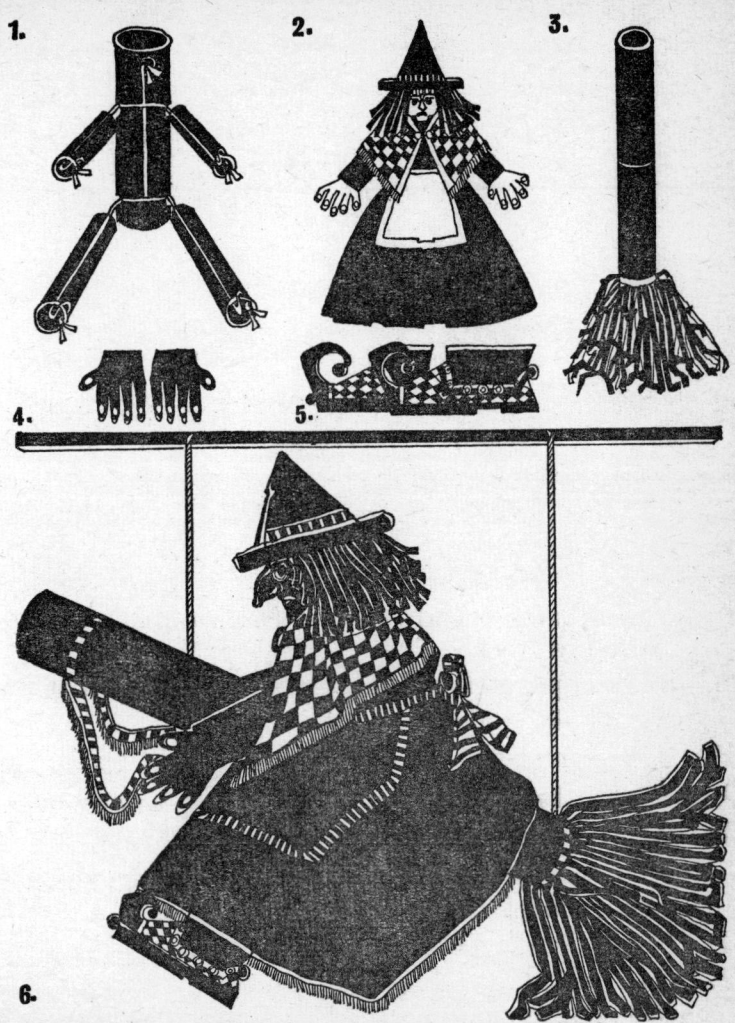

6.

Using cardboard rolls

A Rocket

A. Take a large round cardboard roll to make the lower part of the rocket.

B. Shape a piece of card into an open-ended cone to make the middle section.

C. Take a smaller cardboard roll to make the top part.

D. Fix the three parts together firmly with sticky tape.

E. Cut pieces of card into squares to make the supports, and glue them into position, large ones at the bottom and smaller ones for the top part.

F. Now paint the rocket.

G. The 'lift' at the side is made with a long thin cardboard roll. The passages are made of cut paper and are glued across the 'lift' and on to the rocket.

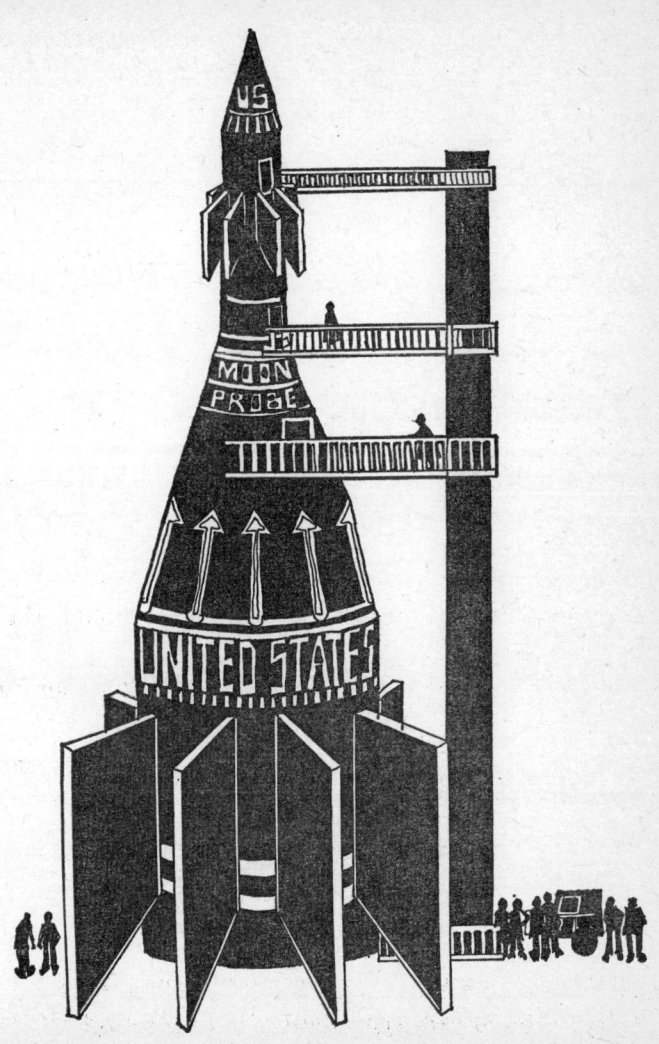

Using cardboard rolls

A Creature From Outer Space

A. Take two shoe boxes and fill them with pebbles to make the feet of the creature. This will also help the model to stand up.

B. Use two more shoe boxes to make the legs, and on top of these glue a stout piece of cardboard.

C. Take a number of rolls, sticking them together with sticky tape, and attach them with glue and tape to the sheet of cardboard.

D. Make sure there is one roll at the top to make the head.

E. For the arms make small holes in the top rolls on each side through which pieces of thin wire can be tied.

F. Hands made of paper cut-outs can be attached to the wire arms.

G. Now paint the creature. You can use dressmakers' pins or hairpins for some of the 'spikey' bits on the head and legs and feet.

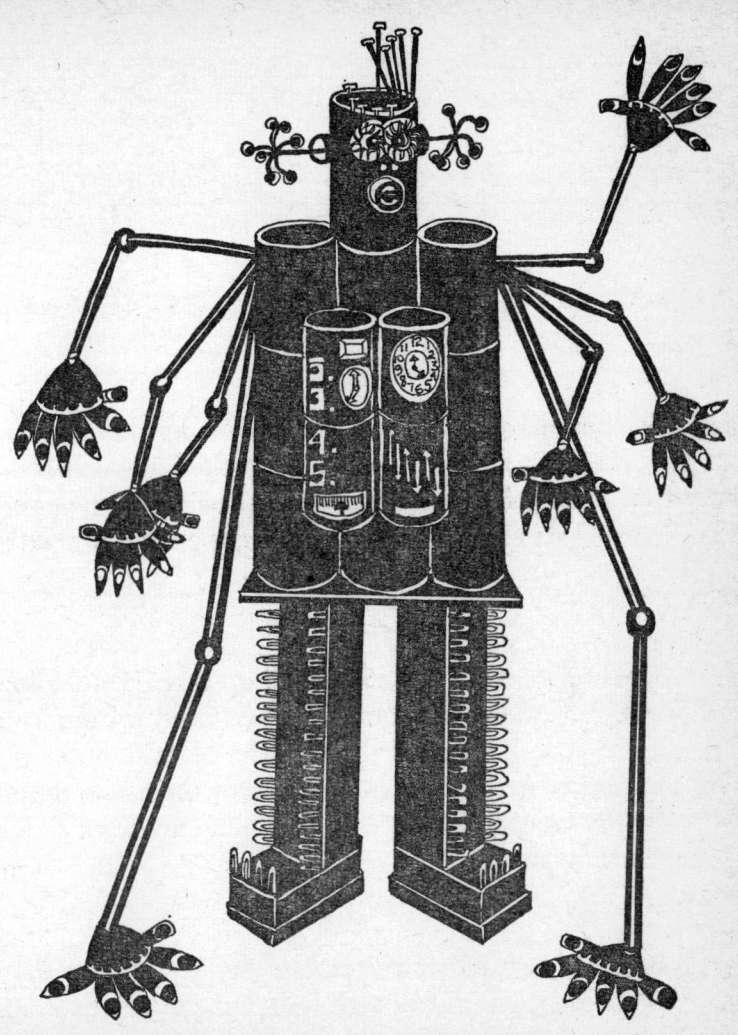

Using paper plates

Hats

Each of these hats is made with an ordinary paper plate.

Hat A
The fruit is made by cutting out the 'fruit' shape in firm card and painting it in bright colours. Glue the fruit on to the plate. Two pieces of ribbon are sewn to the sides of the paper plate. When these are tied under the chin, the hat is shaped to the head.

Hat B
In this hat the rim of the plate is turned up to make a shallow bowl shape. The flowers are made of coloured tissue paper and thin wire can be pushed through the plate to make the stems. A piece of net is sewn to the front of the hat so that it will cover the face, and two pieces of ribbon are sewn to the sides as for Hat A.

Hat C
This is made of two paper plates, one slightly smaller than the other, which are glued together. Flower patterns are painted on the top plate and ribbons added as for the other hats.

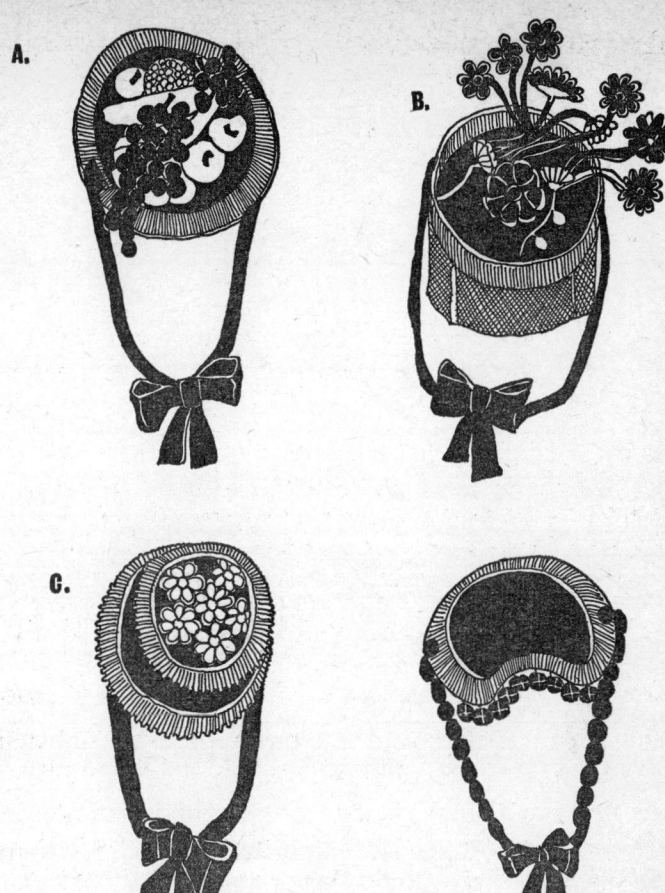

A.

B.

C.

D.

Hat D

This hat is the simplest of all to make. The plate is bent in the front as shown in the diagram. Milk bottle tops are sewn on to this shaping making a sort of fringe. The ribbons are made of fabric scraps.

Using paper plates

An Indian Wigwam

A. Take a paper plate and cut out a piece as shown in diagram 2.
B. Fold the plate to make a cone shape as in diagram 3. Use sticky tape (on the inside and outside of the cone) to secure it. You could use staples or pins.
C. Cut a triangular shape to make the opening of the wigwam.
D. Fold back the rim of the plate and use drawing pins to hold it firmly to the base.
E. Now paint patterns on the tent.
F. The head mask could be made out of clay or Plasticine or cut out of card and decorated with feathers.

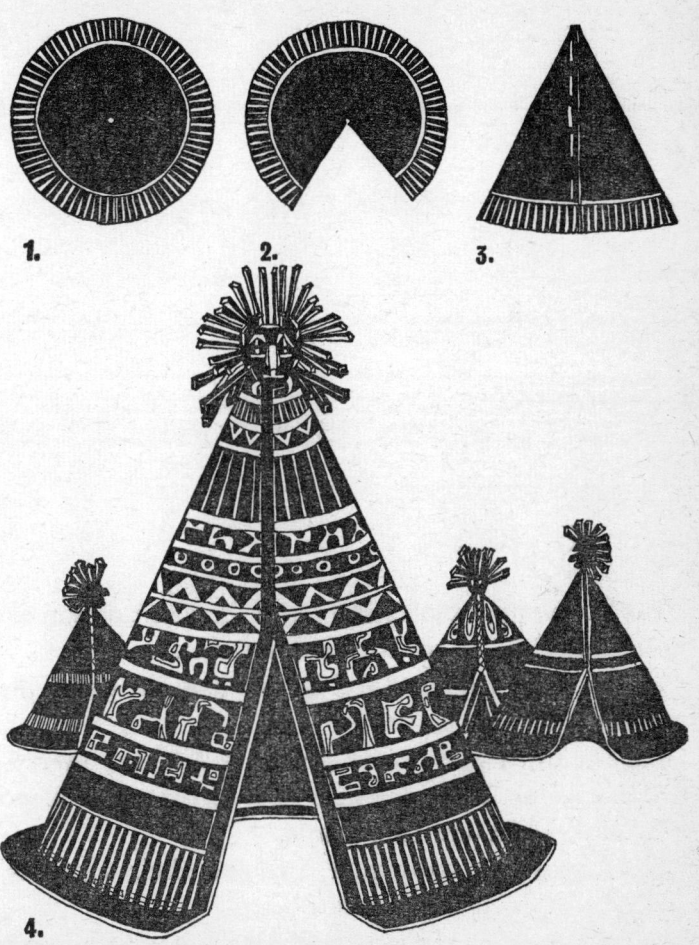

1.

2.

3.

4.

Using paper plates

A Merry-Go-Round

A. Take two paper plates and place them one on top of the other as shown on the base of diagram 1.

B. Take a thin cardboard roll and fix it to the paper plates with sticky tape.

C. Take a third plate to make the top of the merry-go-round frame, cutting a hole in it so that the roll pokes through. Fix it with sticky tape.

D. Now draw the individual cars and their supports on firm card. Paint and decorate them.

E. Cut out these card shapes and fix them with sticky tape to the top plate.

1.

2.

3.

Other non-fiction titles in the same series

The Zebra Book of Facts for Boys
The Zebra Book of Facts for Girls
The Zebra Book of Games and Puzzles
The Second Zebra Book of Games and Puzzles
My History of Music
The Zebra Dictionary in Colour
The Zebra Cook Book
Ask Me A Question
The Zebra Outdoor Book
The Zebra Indoor Book